# Love Hurries This

hamish guthrie

AT BAY press
WINNIPEG

Love Hurries This



Design and layout by Matthew Stevens and M. C. Joudrey.

Published by At Bay Press November 2022.



Library and Archives Canada cataloguing in publication is available upon request.

ISBN 978-1-988168-67-8

Printed and bound in Canada.

This book is printed on acid free paper that is 100% recycled ancient forest friendly (100% post-consumer recycled).

First Edition

10 9 8 7 6 5 4 3 2 1

atbaypress.com

# Love Hurries This

For Terri

and her parents and mine

**CONTENTS**

## ACKNOWLEDGMENTS

I want to express my warmest thanks to my publisher, Matt Joudrey, who first believed in this collection, and to my editor, Karen Clavelle, for her constant support and encouragement throughout the work on the manuscript and the creativity and inspiration in her suggestions.

Some of the poems in this collection appeared in the following publications:

*Acta Victoriana, The Antigonish Review, The Cape Rock, Contemporary Verse 2, Daybreak, The Dalhousie Review, Descant, The Fiddlehead, Grove, indirections, The Malahat Review, Museletter, The New Quarterly, Niagara Anglican, Once in a Sycamore, Pennine Platform, Poem, Poetry Canada Review, Poetry East, Poetry Toronto, Prairie Fire, Propaganda, Queen's Quarterly, The South Carolina Review, The South Dakota Review, Water, Weber Studies, Wisconsin Review, The Yale Literary Magazine.*

The following poems appeared in *Crosscurrents,* ed. Robyn Sarah, Cormorant Books (2011): "Christmas," "The Bubble's Hold," "A Road Near Kosovo," "Geography," "In Country Near Elora," "The Afterlife," "The Castle," "Night Fishermen on Bronte Pier," and "Noise."

## THE HAMMOCK

Here you read
the under-writing
of the leaves
in a cradle
of hours.
You feel
the blue importance
of the sky.
You face up to it.
You are
out of step
with the house
all afternoon.
You lie
in an effortless
cloth wing.
A million leaves
close over you,
like the eyelids
of the sun.

## A MAP OF GRASS

Summer unsettled us.
Birds watched the chaos
of the first blue house
we tied down, flapping,
in the middle field.
The first path
to the river
crossed a crumbled fence.
Our feet mapped grass.
We neighboured bees and moths.
Butterflies stopped
on the fat green pods
of milkweed.
Yellow finches candled
the green cedars.
Alfalfa turned purple.
We kettled fire
sometimes in a soup of rain.
Owls watched stealing moles
and mice.
Night walks carried
the moon's kerosene.
The stars went out with us.
Cotted at night,
we zippered sleep.
Mornings gauzed
the river's surface
We walked down to white mist.

## DOAD GOW

Nothing moved him faster than a crawl
in his old green truck, a big man hunched
at the wheel who took his time.
Two maiden sisters in the house, unpainted,
weathered boards, on the Queen Mary Road,
aged with him, greying ever nearer stone.
He moved like his name,
two long vowels in the throat
of the concession roads.

He turtled to his work, the county dump,
managed that fenced cavity in the hill,
posted dangers and working hours,
decided depths and opened new ground,
accepting to their burial, all things
broken, rusted, empty, smashed,
from nearby farms and cottages.
He was the mortician of beds and chairs
and stoves. The service, fire and ash,
closed on the hour, three strands of wire
on poles he stretched across the lane.

He knew the muddy fields, shallow creeks
and sullen weather, a sardonic, sluggish
smile spread warmly for a muttered joke.
We knew his truck: we knew his name.
Passing us walking, he always stopped,
and dropped us nearer, if not home.
I sometimes wonder if he ever raced
for girls or bars or some other delinquency.
Whatever my speculation, he was faithful
to his dark hill and the old green truck.
His old face told my questions not to dig.
He lived to keep the secrets of his hill.

## FENCING

The trouble with that quiet place
was neighbours butting heads.
The feeling went to ground
across a fence.

A pond can hate a field
when teal are flying.
Barbed wire is an implication
hunters cross.

One bloody morning
the business was the fence
my father wanted
against these guns.

He and Dale walked to the line
and started.
Scrub to be cleared.
My father swung the bright axe high.

Bending a sapling for the blade,
Dale leaned too close.
The axe came down
on the side of his skull.

Blackbirds screamed.
Dale slumped. He moaned.
His red blood pooled
on the grass.

My father walked him out,
half carrying him,
both too white with shock

to tell what had happened.

Our neighbour here was death
that did not cross.
The stitches healed
like the fence.

The teal have come back.
Across the tightened wire,
the pond and the field
both look at the sky.

## IN COUNTRY NEAR ELORA

The air is the breath
of tomatoes and timothy grass.
A stream divides cattle pasture
from fields. The water slows
at a pool and goes under the road
where red-winged blackbirds
in the reeds chatter and fuss.

On circling currents hawks rise and decline.
The hills are heavy with corn and dust.
White butterflies migrate across alfalfa.
Cattle turtle into the shade.

The lane falls asleep at noon.
It waits beside the barn
for the bone white footsteps of the moon.

## BLUE HERON

Ghostly, it makes its haunt
the bogs and creeks, gaunt
as a tamarack, its wings
and back the soft dull colour
mist puts on the water.
Long legs pretend to be shadows
of reeds in the shallows.

Stillness is a thin disguise.
Startled, it will rise, lunging
in distress and
awkwardness, wild with fright,
until wings reach safe height.
Distant, nothing moves from place to place
with motions of such grace.

The time to watch is short
after the wing-beats start.
The bird, beautiful to see,
seeks invisibility. I watch,
and as it glides behind
the trees, the hawthorn at the bend
cuts off the last
glimpse of the river's ghost.

## CHURCHES

Farmers planted faith
when they planted corn.
Wind wrote scripture on their backs
and they believed in rain and bent
to the length of the weather,
measuring Eden to the fence.

A square foundation on the hill
claimed the height with quarried stone.
Sects in diversity arrived,
took up horse and plow,
harrowed each allotted plot,
and churches rose from the fields.

A rivalry of spires and bells
built new pulpits in the town
before it was a town, and the air cleaved
to the Babel of horses and hammers,
axes and wagons at work
interpreting the wilderness.

Labour paid a holy mortgage
with savings from the sheaves,
a treasure laid up from the fields.
Thick shoulders gathered to themselves
for the repeated texts
and stories of the settled earth.

Called into the fields
before the sun was up,
they worked late into the shadows,
rested and sanctified rest,
rested like birds on a spire
and in a corner of the field.

## ALL MY JUNK

Down cellar steps,
in a room he built for me,
I lived under everyone,
under the press and creak
of steps across my ceiling roof.

I lived below the voices.
I heard things moving over me,
felt moods shift upstairs
while I was under them.
His voice came down to me.

Then he himself came down,
Polyphemus with his stick
shouting family law at the mess,
my unmade bed, clothes, books, shoes, skates,
magazines, hockey pads – all my junk.

And it was hell all Saturday,
trapped. So bad I cried, and stayed
in the tidied room he wanted, crying
until my mother called us
out of this to lunch.

In the empty dining room
I surfaced for my soup.
He was reading elsewhere. He called,
said he'd heard I needed hockey gloves.
His changed mood was another tidying.

I did. Next day I wore
the apology he did not say.
My father was the leather on my grip,

my pride in the fast, rough game,
the sheath on my fist.

## CANDY

You taught me the law can happen at midnight
because that was when I came to you and confessed.

Up from my basement room to you at the party
I said I had stolen some candy that afternoon
from Paul's on the corner and had run away.

I couldn't sleep with the sweetness.

You taught me the law pays debts,
puts on a coat immediately,
and leaves the party.

There was a mirror in the store
where I admitted this. You let me hang
in front of myself until the truth eased.

And you let me find my feet beside you
going home to sleep –

to certainty I could taste.

## BOTTLES

He nursed my father back
from long grey days that went to feed
the mortgage on the little rooms
where we were growing up.

He tipped my father from his mood
like straight Scotch splashed in a glass.
He lived two doors down from us
as near as family.

Insurance man,
and practical as doors,
he knew the business that sat down
inside my father,

when he needed out
of those days,
and arguments
you never win at home.

He was the bank
my father borrowed from.
He had better tools than a shop
and he knew how.

My father made an evening of the need,
a drink, another joke, the tool,
and sometimes it was just
an hour out of the house.

His house was as cramped,
and looked at the same street,
but he knew the things

my father couldn't feel at home.

I liked my father more
when he came home from this,
as if he had been far away,
unbottled, bottled, borrowed and returned.

## DUO

The elder of the two sisters wore a small brown stole
around her throat, a fox:
we studied legs with claws and pointed ears

and small glass eyes when she walked past.
This stopped our hockey in the street to watch.
We made a game of her

going somewhere safe and careful like the bank,
this small brown furry death on her.
We loved the mimic and the mockery

that hammered up a fence against these two,
our sneers like nails. We feared the trespass if our games
should cross the bristled lawn they kept,

the sting of their watching silence,
our clatter and shouts the very opposite of linens
and crinolines that dozed.

Hot days, they lived behind green canvas awnings lowered
against the sun. Their quiet needed dark.
In summer, in the lulls in our noise,

we sometimes heard the sisters murmur on the porch,
low sounds like prayer.
For hours they never moved.

## KAPUSKASING

A few short hours must shrink
the distance to a logging town
five hundred miles up north, and link
that place on roads unknown
where they have gone to live
into the family.
My brother and his wife arrive
from holidays in Germany.
A sample story: sampling five
or six strange beers, and we begin
on other news they have:
a bottle of Eiswein.
Dinner talk must taste all this,
reach out five hundred miles from us,
and drag that logging town down close.

It's warm, and I suggest
a walk beside the lake before
they go, and so the rest
of their time's spent down beside the shore.
Bill hunts for skipping stones.
I sit and watch him pick
the pebbly beach for ones
with weight and shapes he likes,
then send the smooth wave-polished shale
miles out, time after time, until
dusk, and the landward breeze is cool.

When they went north, they went equipped
with books, and what you learn
about the bush in schools, except
how loneliness can turn
the woods you love into a place you hate.

It tightens like a skidder's chain,
and days become a weight
that drags you to the phone.
Bill sometimes hates his work,
so going back is hard. At eight
they're gone. The truck
goes skipping north tonight
from town to little town,
until bush swallows them,
as lake waves swallow skipping stones.

## RIVER HOCKEY

Ice lured us
under the bridge
when winter sealed
the river's skin.

Woollen fish,
we jumped and swam,
and skates were fins
on the snow-frothed stream.

Hours flurried by.
The loose puck raced
skittered and twirled
like nibbled bait.

All day our wind-mad
school of scarves,
flicking tails,
flapped out behind.

## THE CASTLE

The road he took
from an ancient city
was longer and more difficult
than marked on the maps:
the curling route to the coast,
the sudden jump across the Atlantic.
Arrival was a long descent;
his clothes weren't right for the climate.
He looked back too often
for escape to be easy, and stones
of the old city became things he carried.
Memory took him back to flagstoned chambers
and lifted down the trophies on the walls.
Sickness sometimes affects rough settlements
in a new country, and he was not immune.
The past, like a virus in his blood, gave him
a fever like the illness bones take
from cold stone buildings. He described
the dogs he followed on the Braid Hills,
the tents he pitched at Comrie, fires
where the boy poached kippers.
He needed the rain where he was born,
the rock that choked the centre of that city,
wet roads he walked to school. In his head
photographs we could not see
divided him from us.
When I was born, I was the son
he could not show his father.
I feared the castle that he left
as a cold place locked in his head.
I looked for the door he had opened
when he left, and could not close.

## THE NIGHT HE DIED

The room was like a place prepared
for January, the snowy night he died,
the iron month of his birth.
The clock crawled coldly,
his head on the pillow,
a print in a white drift.
In the bone-coloured room,
in privacy, we watched the slipping
worsen, the doctor letting things fall
out of his hands. Whispers gave
clear, brief reports.
And then the doctor, as if the matter
were routine, finally left himself,
and we watched my father, his head,
his closed eyes, his hands,
and his warm, red blood,
accept the pure transfusion of white snow.

## DECEMBER 21

Nothing disturbs
the room we're in
and this last time
I have with him.

Machines are off,
the watching done,
and the screens blank
electric stones.

Routine goes down
the corridors
and doctors go
to other doors,

this night that I
must understand
the pallor on
my brother's hands.

## FOR EMILY ON THE DEATH OF HER BROTHER

The family is weeping, and the priest
in guttural Armenian, attempts
his steady arguments to nurse belief
in skeptics given heavy evidence.
Nothing cauterizes a suicide,
the mouth of the new wound hanging open,
and fingers without skill to work inside
to clean or close the sores that death begins.
The funeral's attention to the corpse
files like a sick-bed watching past your ache
that lies so still, in peace that brings no peace.
Talking will not shorten the time this takes.
If only medicine had hands to press
the pulse out of such grief and helplessness.

## THE MOON IN THAT COLD PLACE

In winter the park turned white,
a small white island at the end of the street.
On one side, in the open air,
the gleam of two smooth skating rinks.
One for hockey, the other, cuffed with snow,
invited the infinite circles a day could make
on the open surface of the ice.

Cold evenings, coming from the trains,
people crossed the path in thinning crowds.
I liked to come here later by myself
when I had closed my books and notes,
shut Hegel and John Stuart Mill,
and hushed Kant and Donne.
I wanted darkness and night sky
and silences to clear my head.
Sometimes I walked and sometimes I ran
to clear the fever of my spinning head
to the bench where I laced up my skates.
I had the ice completely to myself,
to spin poems and philosophy asleep.

Saturdays were carnivals of scarves
and hats and coats and woollen mitts
and beginners pushing chairs
between the legs of their mothers.
Fathers bent to collect the falls
and rubbed and soothed bumped heads.
They lifted little ones from accidents.
The sun cast a light like summer
on the frozen slickness of the sheet,
and games of tag and stolen hats
raced across the ice on this

cold tumble of a winter day.

Night shuttered the rinks
because there was no electric light
except the one high beacon on the path.
It was yellow and wan in the cold,
a light for night birds in the naked trees.

Pick-up games were like a fever in the snow.
Saturday mornings weltered and seethed,
a rabble that scrambled in scrimmages
between unpainted hemlock boards, and the goals
were naked steel frames frozen in the ice.
Games were strung out in the weather
and sometimes lasted into storms,
the puck like a jumping mouse in the snow.
But at night the rinks were dark:
parka-wrapped skaters and teams long gone
dissolved away into the snowy streets.
The night that looked back to the rink, watched
from apartments and warm curtained rooms.
Soft lights glowed in windows.
No one came to the park except
late walkers with their dogs
and they crossed quickly to get home.

At night I loved this open emptiness,
skeletal trees and dark doorways,
snow-hatted roofs and the leaning fence,
the wind that rattled the hairy willows,
the dark quietness and vacancy.
I loved the moon because it added light,
a whiteness on the whiteness of the snow.
I stepped to feel the blades' brisk scratch.
I wanted away from my room and books,
sentences and trailing arguments,

to rest in the slide of the ice.
My skates etched lines under the hanging moon.
Mine was the roving coated shadow
under the fixtures of the bony trees.
I moved away from what I brought
to the counterpoint of skates.
Under an open sky
I read the easy pages of the wind.

I wanted the air to think of a girl
whose house was a tangent to the park,
and tangent to my circles on the ice.
Her house was near the corner
where mornings she would catch the bus
to school that lifted her to music and the stage.
Coincidence and chance both jumped.
We met one morning,
years after I had watched her
sitting on the other side of the class,
and for a time, things smiled. I learned
the worries, dreams and plans she found
in her frenetic orchestra.
And she loved the Russian language so one night
at a movie I brought a book
of Voznesensky's poems, a favourite
for a favourite, and watched
her small white fingers moving on the words
and the translation on her lips.

I followed her, invited to the spectacle
of light and dance in which she moved,
her life in music and the lifted steps.
I looked for Giselle because I glimpsed her,
lived for the warm light in what I saw,
the dancer's leap and lifted, reaching fire.
The moon in that cold place

was near enough to feel
the music holding her.

They were only possibilities,
shadows and the shadow of myself
not lucky or fast enough
to catch a chance before it disappeared.
I warmed to what I couldn't hold.
Circles rounded on the ice in emptiness
under the moon. I laughed at myself
and hoped that things would change.
They didn't and they did.

## JUNE

Another lazy sunset on the edge
of the escarpment drags the June day down,
and puts on fields new green a yellow tinge.
The sun makes this finale all her own.
Light spills and seeps, and the experience
is walking through a doorway to the west,
an orange room, that offers no defence
to strangers, or to any seeking rest.
The evening holds things still, can hypnotize
to motionless the trees, the hawk, the wind,
exerts this force on human thought and eyes.
Political, would make a king rescind
his wishes, schemes and lies. And so the trees
stand, overcome by yellowness and ease.

## CAT AFTER DARK

She goes out smoothly
like slow grey mist at dusk

unpools from the pillow
on the lamplit bed,

and pours herself
descending the stairs

seal-smooth, dark shining
on the carpeting.

She ripples herself along the corridor,
water-like, for silence

out the door.
In the becalmed front garden

she is a ripple under the hedge,
a liquid moving on the grass,

a splash against car tires on the drive.
When the wind is nothing

she goes up over the fence
sudden as spray on a rock.

She drowns the things she hunts.

## TWO WHITE CHAIRS

Near the centre
of the cafe
two white chairs
face each other

suggesting
the girl and boy
who faced each other
before they left.

## YELLOW FLOWERS

On my table
a glazed blue vase
swells, tightens
and then opens

like a horn
blowing yellow flowers,
the incarnation of sound.

## I CUT THE WEEDS

I cut the weeds around the ditch,
churned into noise and blue gas fumes
alfalfa, daisies, berry vines,
and long hay grass the rain made rich.
The place, to the suburban eye,
looked much, much better after this
rough mulching into what would please
a neighbour's sense of symmetry.
Finished, I thought it wastefulness
to treat the garden as I had.
I know that the mosquitoes bred
a nuisance in the ditch-side grass,
but I missed colours thrashed to ruin
where soft July gave ragged bloom.

## ONE SUNDAY MORNING

Out on our bicycles we wandered
down long tunnel-dark ravines
descending cool dark paths,
the woodland's winding passages,
paths that licked the edges of a creek,
the shadows, and the watered stones.

We went where aged willows leaned
across a shallow stream, light sifting
through the leaves in airy places, in
gaps between the trees, where gardens were
nests and houses slept like resting moths,
stone steps descending
the round shoulder of a hill.

We took a tented path between
columns of giant ash and birch and oak.
Photographs could not have seen what
progress we made, our backs patched
by shade and dappled light,
under the breathing cover of a leafy mesh.

Water ahead, we pushed on
to come to it, to the moment
when the dark tunnel ends,
when the lake bursts open
to the wide blue glare
of sunlight on a hammered plate.

## KILLARNEY LAKE

We pitch a collapsible neighbourhood
in a niche on the rocks
and hang bright colours,
socks and towels on ropes.
We people the trees with clothes.

Dawn is a blush on the nylon tent.
Noon burns bald rocks.
Dark is a festering of flies,
a glum thickening in the sky
that sinks the moon.

Roofed by spruce, we study clouds
distrustfully. Rain falls
through the fingers of the trees.

We notice layers in the rocks,
uneven bands across the hills,
and fear the heaving eons
that pushed hills at the sun
like froth on boiling tea.

Sleep here is fitful, slung
in the geography of dreams
on strange, uneven ground.

## THE PIER

Old boats weighed anchor here, in Parry Sound,
plied these islands and the channel
and tied up at the pier,
steel boats, ore boats, steamers,
fishing trawlers, yachts.
The summer I worked in town,
a white yacht from the Caribbean
wanted crew for a year –
paid room and board.
I had turned eighteen. I dreamed
of sails for university, a wind
out of my father's reach, instructions
taken from the stars
in their fixed distances,
from mapped constellations
and the charts
of deep water, near the sun.
I applied for this in dreams,
and was accepted into the swift
uncertainties of the boat,
days over the keel
always cutting its course
to remote islands,
and sleep, for months,
in the cabin of my studies,
on streets over fish,
carried, tilting, south,
on the wrinkled sea.

## GEOGRAPHY

I hear he's failed Geography.
The rivers of the world
run on in emptiness to him,
and all the complicated names
for rock are meaningless.

But I have seen him, slouching at his desk,
open chasms in himself like continents,
oblivious to me or anyone.
He's learned the way
the heart of things can boil
and harden into shape,
how islands are defined.
He's felt words like a river's push
gain force and
carry everything away.

His white *Crown Royal* baseball cap
screens more than rain or sun.
But I have seen him sit for half an hour
with a book about a boy
whose family is broken into splinters
of grey rock, and read until
he finds a place inside the world
and one long river that he knows.

## AN EXPERIENCE THAT CHANGED ME

She sets her composition down for English class,
reveals one problem of her sallow face,
a blue exhaustion deeper than fatigue
that rings her eyes and sleeps in her
every day she is awake.

She puts this down in paragraphs,
in the hushed room, sitting,
by a fluke, closest to the door.
Brushing back her long fair hair
to clear the page, she writes,
in the time they have,
*An experience that changed me.*

I get to it a week later, after
she's missed two days, been late, I've wondered
why no one answers when I phone.
She writes the story of her father's suicide.
I learn the ache of memory that's hers,
that lies behind her mornings before me,
learn why even silence troubles her.
Words, like a daughter's arms,
heavy with memory, reach out into death.

## UP

One piece Phil wrote describes the night
he and a buddy climbed on the roof of the school
and sat to smoke a cigarette.

I picture them, feet dangling happily over the edge,
safe, in this danger, from detection,
kept secret, at least from me, until
confession in reckless spelling,
for credit in the class.

He crows about the night they sat on top
of everything. My comments touch on grammar,
details in description, spelling, and commend
the energy and length he gives to
how he broke school rules
his sentences forget.

I keep to what is happening with his pen.
I want him to enjoy the warm night picture of himself,
do justice to the crazy friend up there with him,
describe the moon and everything he saw
dangling there.

I want him to enjoy the night's grin in the sky.

## THE GIRL FROM SERBIA

I remember the curve of her back to her book,
a beige beret pulled almost to her ears,
the P.A.'s foreign jangle in the class,
her *Hamlet* open, her whispering lips.
A joke could capture her entire face,
dissolve the sleepless worry from her eyes,
the daily clutch at notes on Shakespeare's play.
The teacher's dream, a girl who longed to learn,
no use for anything except her books,
no changing, daily, bright experiments,
the face she wore entirely her own.

I tried to tell her she should stay in school,
live with her uncle when her parents move
to a big new house, but fifty miles away –
complete the course. Tears filled her eyes.
I sensed more problems than I knew.
She's shown me glimpses of the home she left.
I've learned the amputations of her life,
ambitions cut by war in Serbia,
dreams she took from her grandmother's work,
studying psychiatry and making books
her life, not the vagabond's broken path
and losses exile imposed.

I think of her careful sentences,
the pained correction of her words,
the sounds she reached to use,
her need to make speech accurate,
the warm and open features of her face,
grasping things in through a web,
pulling English over distances.
A concentrated corner of the room

is empty, and it suffers,
as if its keenest nerve were cut.

## A QUESTION FOR THE SKY

I wonder where he's lounging now, Nick,
who lounged against the cupboards here,
but started class with a shout,
a fist of a kid from a farm,
who hated his Dutch father,
and came to school for relief
from fights at home and downtown,
and things I only guessed.

One day at my desk, he said *I can't do this*,
and why – *because my brother's being sentenced today,*
*and I don't even know where I am.*
I let him lounge, and never learned
the verdict then, on his brother, or Nick,
who broke school rules like glass
and got cooled out
by a vice-principal regularly.

Nick slipped out
between the bars of policy,
his graduation one last broken ultimatum.
And there are vacancies that bring him back,
laughter louder than rules,
big shoulders that won't lift books.
I lapse and wonder where he leans,
or what he's bent against, shouting about,
if there are ears across the air.

## ESPERANZA

I look up from my papers
when she comes in
glad of the quiet
and the empty desks.

Curious about her Spanish accent
I want to know the story
and when I ask,
she tells me why she left El Salvador.

She spreads a continent across the classroom,
and across the afternoon as she speaks
and she rides in her brother's truck
where traffic is congested with soldiers
out of the city into hot dry hills and
mountains I have never seen.
Escape reaches Houston and works
further north to Ontario.

She laughs at the end as if she can't believe it.
My questions have taken her back to
the twists of childhood bells in cathedrals
the crack of guns and poverty like faith
where many kneel.

When she is finished
she smiles and settles
in the room that holds her story –
and together we can feel
there is nothing at all to fear
in the wind in the leaves outside the window.

## *IN MEMORIAM*

for Terrence Bredin

Much mimicked mimicker, old polyglot,
grammarian, and cricketer, you teased
us through the books of Homer's plot,
Odysseus yourself the waters pleased
to wash to us as if to Ithaca,
a place you also made a bookish Rome.
And so, I happened to meet Nausicaa
floating with you those wayward waters home.
You took us from brass rubbings and the glut
of cluttered shelves to read under the trees,
to open Homer by the cricket hut.
Odysseus made progress by degrees
that wandered sometimes from his wanderings,
out on the grass in May to other things.

## ANCIENT HISTORY

The years of cigarettes had thinned the frame
that moved his smoky grey tweed jacket
along the aisles, the cold linoleum,
a distance from the Sphinx. This was the place
to question pharaohs. Notes disturbed the dust.
The afternoon's declension numbered down
the causes of Rome's fall; our hands,
fatigued and fisted, followed after him,
those heavy hours, through empires,
dynasties, and all the broken cities
he chronicled, the favourite ghosts
we dreaded on exams, but he would not
let Janus' backward progress flinch.
So, history dogged the year in our reports:
he worried us with failing centuries.
He taught my uncle. My last
warm afternoon at the school,
new graduate, I saw him on the grounds,
too old to remember me, I thought.
But he did. We talked. Then I shook
his nicotine-yellowed hand and he closed
the door that closed the epoch of his talk.

## MARK TWAIN

Because Mark Twain was watching, looking down
at me, I feared my teaching could be wrong
unless it heard the skeptic in the room
who might not give a damn for anything.
That was the warning always on the wall,
Twain's face pinned up to teach me Huck was there –
or should be, or was late, or like them all,
was watching some strange something at the door
and Shakespeare wouldn't likely bring them back.

Twain liked a kind of half-unruly class:
the little careful things some parents like
in detail, taught, reviewed, to get a pass
would never land a fish, make friends, or swim.
His watching bothered my curriculum.

## THE MAN WHO HATED GOVERNMENT

Three hundred pounds, he gossiped and blasphemed,
bloody to his elbows with the work
of hacking carcasses to chops of good red meat.
He spattered his opinions round the room,
cursed, laughed and stabbed at fools,
his meat-block a judge's bench,
the capitol of comment in the town.
His customers were friends for life,
ignored the chain next door
that tried to buy him out.
Take forty years of orders on the phone,
you learn enough to curse and be believed
about the troubles in a northern town.

He hated government because
he knew no better law than need,
like his own father's exiled start
from Italy, bound for Thunder Bay,
heading for a place he didn't know,
the town's name pinned to him,
with nothing else for help the day he docked,
as speechless as the baggage from the hold.

He muscled cans by armloads from his truck,
lugged the cardboard boxes
to the porches of the town,
down alleys to the kitchen doors.
A voice like Moses, he arrived,
the sound of a shout in all he said,
and the big man's hot chain-smoker's doubt
was better than the manna in his hands.

## MRS. GILLMOR

She was a landmark, like her house,
widow, eccentric Scot, warm great lady,
who made her big house our revolving residence:
Cairncross who taught French, two girls from Kaladar
and me, a waif from the train, to work the summer in town.

Presbyterian and categorical, she was
a clamp on her Bible and its commandments,
generous to confusion, kind, gentle, adamant,
but when she locked her door, the wind came in.
Her fridge swelled like a full-bellied whale,
and sickened with frugality; cheese bits she saved,
half-apples, pickles, meats well-wrapped for tomorrow
turned the colour of disease. There were questions
put to all of us, disavowals; dishes of green loss.

Her husband's hardware store provisioned the town.
Her memory rattled like a box of nails.
She fabled the nights her son climbed out his window
to meet the Ukrainian girl fear wouldn't bring home
to meet his Scottish parents.
She laughed at herself and her principles,
and her beloved son married his secret.

Booze at the end was revelation, a translation.
Dressed in her best for the purchase,
as if for church, she walked the cracked pavement stones
and briskly, to meet the nice man at the store.
Scotch tipped the house. We heard her rummage
in the cupboard for the bottle that defeated
absent sons. She poured herself downstairs
to the bottom where she did not know us
or the reason for the ambulance.

We called her son in Minneapolis for help, to the house,
the house where years had whitened her laughter,
and would not let her sleep.

## KENNY

I remember him on a ladder,
mornings working on the engine of a Norseman,
long, grease-blackened arms reaching into
problems that pulled the bush-plane
from the water. Curses and cigarettes
made a good beginning.
Sweat in the hangar had nothing to do
with trout, or yellow pickerel, or bass,
but his imagination reached the lakes.

He was happiest bent double in the guts
of an aluminum bird, a spanner in his hand,
a gauge or pliers, feeling for loose wires,
nursing dead cylinders back to flight, his cheeks
pressed like a kiss on a malingering motor.
His quick, raw laugh made a fifteen-minute break
a stove in a storm. The table settled to his grin.
I liked him best when coffee and a smoke
spilled a wreck out
of his cup, a crash and recovery
happened again, some madness
died in a cabin, or a kid pilot
panicked, dropped too fast
glassy water grabbed the floats –
the plane somersaulted and sank.

Flight, for him, was never higher
than his ladder. Coffee, then back up
to his fishing. He put his hands in the deep
water, where the lunkers idled,
a mind for the cold bottoms
and weather. Finished, he came down.
He rubbed his hands with a rag.

He laughed and left the pilot
his beginnings: the propellor's cough.

## A DEATH AT COUCHICHING

Midnight rings at different hours
in the jumbled pink and blue cabins
on rocky hills near the tracks
that bend around the bay.

Alarms go off when the bars close.
Limits break in a little town.
What happens on the fast roads home
to families in shacks is chased and taken down
in detail by the OPP.

The kid had his blaster in his ear.
He left the bar and walked
out of town, on the tracks.
The train caught up to him.

Riding my bicycle in the morning
I pass the aftermath,
the train – stopped there,
a huge beast, stunned
by what it has done,
and people standing around
helping the sun to come up.

Gossip in coffee shops accepts the news.
The weekly paper reports a burial,
a service closes the grave,
and memory fails slowly after the accident.
A cabin on the rocks is dark.

At night the silent moon
lays one straight silver track
across the lake.

## THE WHITE PINE BAR

When darkness closed the seaplane bases on the bay
and every tourist fisherman was home
or ferried to a lake up north, pilots
and mechanics, halfway home, drank here.
They left the lakes to whoever wanted them,
fish to the stories that caught them, and
drove to sit where they could stop the clock.
In night's forgetfulness, pilots and greasy hands
that nursed dilapidated planes to flight
elbowed to a seat at a favourite table
and beer stains on the garish, patterned rug
in a one-room tavern on the town's main drag
and sat as if they could no longer move.

Talk was the White Pine's menu,
and the bar was a rebuilding shop
where planes came back from doom.
Drowned planes resurfaced from deep lakes,
burst floats resealed, cylinders drained,
and broken instruments replaced.
Dead engines sang in the whine of the sky
and wrecks were birds again.
Bush planes, like mosquitoes, buzzed to lakes
good maps forgot. Flights came home all night.

Talk reached the outer points on memory's charts.
The night ignored the moon,
sneered at the party from Chicago
tomorrow would bring home,
lit up again, and as the waitress laughed,
called for another, and denied they knew
how cold the air can feel at 5 a.m.

## A ROAD NEAR KOSOVO

They walk toward us beside thick trees
along a road the paper says
has emptied fields and towns.
A family, a fragment of the line,
a man and wife, holding between them,
a large cloth bag.

They have clearly only started out.
Nothing has tousled yet
the woman's neat blonde hair,
as chic as if it had been styled today.
Two children run about laughing,
as if the line of their straggling procession
in heat that's stripped an old man to his undershirt,
were a summer excursion and they
were tourists going to a beach.

The camera leaves them
lurching toward what camp they find,
in lightweight shoes and summer clothes
and not much else for the sun
or weather that turns cold –
more days like this ahead,
naked to the stones of shifting policy
and the rains of diplomacy,
between them a large cloth bag getting heavier
with everything they leave behind.

## ALEPPO

This morning, this picture in the paper,
the body of a child uncovered
in the rubble of the city, limp
in the arms of the men who discovered it.

The child's loose hair hangs
from their arms and they stop
for the camera's eye to glimpse
the unblemished face dusted
with the ruin of the city.
Rescuers have paused –
how to continue
after such an unearthing?

It's good the camera was here –
good that the generals
who conducted the destruction
have a picture to document
the proof of victory,
the total silence of the enemy,
eyes and small mouth completely closed,
and the completeness of this grief.

## THE BUBBLE'S HOLD

Inside his jacket a quilt of wires
plugged him into heat
in the tight, clear bubble of the gun at 20,000 feet.
Tonight brings back the sudden fate he wore,
the engine's heavy rumble toward the target,
the anti-aircraft guns that tried to pick a father
out of this mission to a foreign city,
him, eighteen, over Czechoslovakia,
the moment no one could pull out,
the wing-to-wing formation fixed–death
to break it, as easy as the flak through glass.
It held. The sky's fire died.

The story ruined a ball-bearing factory
and carried him to Europe in the belly of a plane
that nightmares crashed
because, warnings to evacuate ignored,
the city, reinforced, fired back.
The odds were even in his dream
but the story stacks the odds for death.
The kitchen counter shatters with black flak.

Something unzipped this tonight.
I try to hear his guns. He lost
the jacket fifty years ago
but the noise comes home:
explosions, and the mercy of the glass
that held him and did not break.

## MUSIC

for John Laing

Wanting only music, he sits to play.
Silence opens like a door. Discord shakes
into the building; pipes, connecting, spray
sound about like a weather he makes
out of the organ. The stone columns feel
increasing wind and rise into storm
and the windows shout as if the building's full
of something that has buried peace and calm.
Arpeggios amalgamate, Bach runs
silver wires to the roof, pedals knock
at the walls, the anthem confabulates, and one
wild glissando, like a chalice, falls and breaks.

## IMPOSSIBLE MUSIC

for Chris Daffef

Toronto bowed him down:
the city gave him work.
On cobbled roads he kneeled
to lay stones in rows,
and then at night
his callused fingers cracked
when he uncased his violin
to practise in a rented room.
He made himself good gloves,
cut uppers off old shoes,
wore soles as mitts.
After his native Hungary, these streets,
and days of impossible music,
his hands at work on stones.

I think it was the stones that made him shout
if my brother would not kneel
to music, if his hands refused to hold
phrases laboured into shape,
if his wrist broke form on the bow
or the violin's smooth neck.
The old man screamed
until his pupil's hands
laid notes in seamless rows,
the music found a way to leave the world
and stones fell from his pupil's hands.

## A SONG FOR BERRYMAN

A wind there came but like a bird he flew
and found a place in cliffs. It rained and rained.
He sang to pass the storm,
and Delmore, Randall, Dylan, men he knew,
danced on with him till only dance remained.
But dancing came to harm.

His fairest song he sang to praise his wife,
And fair the song to Lise, long ago,
the pride of all his art.
But the man of the songs is gone, his life
and dance are done. So said Horatio:
*Now cracks a noble heart.*

He was a prince and brave -
and like a soldier, long as he could be,
like men he envied: Coleridge, Rilke, Poe.
And though he left his end unfinished, he
spanned more bridges than he broke.
*Green they grow, and wide his laurels wave.*

## CABBAGETOWN BALLAD: AFTER HUGH GARNER

*"Anyway, it's gone now, so let's not talk about it*
*on a nice afternoon like this."*
(from Cabbagetown, by Hugh Garner)

She took his arm, and they walked in the park.
  She thought she'd do as he said.
*We still live down on Timothy Place,*
  she said. *That old dump of a house.*
He had called for her at the mansion house
  where she had gone as a maid.
*My mother still drinks the money she gets.*
  *One day it'll kill her, I guess.*
She'd lost her job in the jewellery store
  and took what work she could get.
*I boxed enough soap in that damned factory*
  *to wash half the world if you tried.*

The mansion house made her Cabbagetown slum
  a place she tried to forget.
*You get half your pay for the work you do,*
  *and half because you survive.*
But the mister liked more than the silver's gleam
  and more than the cut of her dress.
*At school I thought I'd be an architect,*
  *got a prize in my drafting class.*
But how could she tell it had broken her heart
  on a nice afternoon like this?
*But that's gone now and let's forget it,*
  *on a nice afternoon like this.*

## SWEET DISORDER: FOR ANNE SEXTON

*"A sweet disorder in the dress*
*Kindles in clothes a wantonness:*
*A lawn about the shoulders thrown*
*Into a fine distraction –*
*An erring lace...*
*Do more bewitch me than when art*
*Is too precise in every part."*
– Robert Herrick

Relaxed and smiling, you lean back at ease,
the famous scholar-poet at her desk.
And resting in your face and eyes there is
a look of un-cosmetic glamour like
the easy confidence an athlete has
when what she does has undergone the check
of measurements, and now is clear as glass.
So, there you rest, your chair tipped back, a glass
half-emptied in your hand, and now permit
neither the worry of love nor of work
to bother you; the moment lets you pause.
Nor can I interrupt here, nor trespass:
your photograph's more private than a book.

Your desk is strewn with papers, hardly neat,
but you had more than house-keeping to do,
and more to put in order than will show.
Your typewriter is there, the instrument
that bore an army of ideas, plans
and prayers. Your desk, more than a birthplace is
an operating table where you salved
and severed, tended, amputated, healed
your wounds and those of others that you took
for them to talk about their pain.

And which is the truer report to take,
the doctor's diagnosis or the howl
of those who feel the cutting of the pain?
Good doctors utter both, feel wounds wide awake,
and learn to know which remedies work best.
You traded wounds for words in every spell,
and paid in patience for each sentence done.
The bargaining was hard; the deal went well.

And here,
you did *The Awful Rowing Toward God.*
You pulled the boat alone a distance out,
with little for a map, no stars about,
no one on board to wake to quell the flood,
and no port very near.

Your mind, by instinct happy, came on doubt,
and poems were your means to search it out.
You knew all hope and doubt, like Simone Weil,
and doubting had the better part of you.
The doubt that broke away inside your heart
performed your poems and required your art.

But you had more to order than we know.
Your God was the awed one out of the world.
To you at work, a mother with her brood,
love sometimes seemed less love than work to do.
You loved, and knew more love than love could tell.
Now I look at this picture of your desk
and search its sweet disorder for a hint
or answer to your secret, deepest, last,
which you could not explain in secret verse.

## EDEN MILLS

in memory of Al Purdy

Somewhere I have a half-drunk autograph
from a summery day in early fall
and readings in a half-wild hillside park,
when you came into the mix.

Announced, you climbed the steps
to the rickety platform,
and behind you, on the creek
a green canoe edged near.

Gaunt and tall, you stood at the podium,
a swag of grey hair, lank,
as always, in your eyes.
We lounged in the grass and weeds,
clouds hanging white in bright weather.
The trees were yellowing,
tenuously bending to cold purposes
even in the day's warm promise.
In the air, words of force and grief.
We wanted you to take longer.

We lounged in the grass and weeds,
under the dying trees, the thrust of your voice
and you leaning into the sound of
the ranging, ragged story of yourself tossed
across the crowd, shouldering out your words
about crossing the white Arctic lament for
lost peoples and wind-carried ghosts
of wilderness, about home, far cities,
and the quirky things life spreads open to your hands,
you, warm in your voice under the trees
and autumn's fiery frail paper roof,

burgundy, ochre, maroon.

You read to the crowd,
and in that jumbled old town
where a watermill died,
everything came back.
But we wanted you to take longer.

Behind you on the creek
that green canoe
floated into what you said.

## LABOUR AND DESIRE

for W. H. Auden

Your labour was the keen desire
to bend art to determine
the shape and feel of ordinary day
and set the landscape in a painted line.

All good work at poetry you considered
an assiduous attempt to diagnose
with keenest instruments
what elsewhere gets contempt
in business and politics –
needs too intimate for applause –

hopes too much like prayer
for hacks to whip into a cause.

Language's authority, you
made the practised revelry
of anthem, sonnet, ballad, ode,
your desk and daily artistry.

You shuffled into the street in slippers
and dishevelled dress, to muse about
in art galleries, re-read the psalms
in New York and London offices,
in Greenwich Village restaurants,
to hear music in common
and uncommon haunts,
in streets that take the world
to their morning faith at eight
in step with doubt and fear
of being late for clockwork employment
linking hands to electric wires

that do not raise a glimmer
from faint desire.

Your mind was gardens, pools,
streets, tombs, grace, a vaulted chapel
holding the longest echoes in
faithless memorial, and belief in the clasp
of intimate hands and lips,
treasures the blind world often
reaches for and trips.

## FOR DEREK WALCOTT

You made the painted island what it was,
taking what came to light: the amber dusk,
the evening's vestiges in villages,
the trees that wore the hanging scent of musk.

You started with the light itself, the light
that washed a coral island and its reach
from headlands and the promontories' height
and felt the urge in seas' repeated touch.

The paper listened where you set your watch.
The sand was printed in the hidden script
of orchids, old towns loosed from empire's clutch,
lost gardens, fertile, deep, half derelict,

shadowed and dark, waiting for you to see
and lift this palette from obscurity.

## LOVE HURRIES THIS

Love hurries this across Montana's hills
to you, two thousand miles three weeks apart,
and running on the mountaintops it tells
you how you fill the hollow of my heart.
Beyond the continent's divide, I set
these words in air, and pray, though I deride
the fear, that we may never want nor let
within us any permanent divide.
In all of this I'm only telling you,
your going darkens our apartment rooms,
in which there's really very little new,
except the violet's twin purple blooms.
These separate flowers represent us two,
and your return, their mixing of perfumes.

## OLD JIMMY

He came in before dark, to look at his shoes
and take his apron off the hook,
Old Jimmy, the night man, in
shuffling steps that came to close the place,
a restaurant beside a public park and pool.
In summer it was busy as a beach resort.
He swept and sang his Greek songs
in a kind of preoccupied oblivion
I interrupted if I needed him.
He smiled at the girls and sat in a chair,
employment more like waiting for a bus.
He locked the place at two. I left at one,
or earlier, released by his nod at the emptiness.
He wiped the tables, wheeled the jukebox in,
and shut the lights, the work that needed only one.

Some nights when the menu was rain,
our work was watching traffic on the street,
or pushing boredom through the hours.
He told me broken stories, half in Greek,
about himself, and real estate he owned and lost,
a house expropriated to build
Summerhill subway station.
Whatever he wanted me to take
from these old griefs and warnings,
I listened to the soft collapse of his talk,
the slow wet nights in the empty place.

One afternoon, the owner's nephew
took me aside, suspiciously, and said,
*Jimmy's stealing. Watch him.* A joke,
I thought. I pictured Jimmy whisking buns
and pickles out the window to a revving truck.

*Watch him.* Of course I didn't. I went home
and left the old man to his mumbled songs,
his losses and the broom, to turn the lock.
I believed the broken things he told me,
though I noticed what was missing,
the nights when he didn't come back.

## NOISE

My neighbour's restless.
He's built a shed, a deck,
and now a wooden fence.
His wild saw screams.
Banging nails annoy the shrieking birds.
Our flowers bloom beside this factory.

I know the reason for his work.
Winter wrecked him twice:
two deaths – his son, by suicide,
and then his brother. We heard
and wondered what grief did,
those slow, grey months inside.

He's making something out of this.
He leans on the fence to talk about his shed,
his metal saw. I'm with the shrieking birds,
but I admire the work I hear,
the nails he buries in new wood
between our properties.

## THE WOODEN HEART

He made a cabinet by touch,
measured each piece
in the dark of his blindness,
set shape in the grain,
knew, exact, each inch
his fingers rubbed
of smooth blond birch.

Most careful artisan,
his hands sent up
the shaped, finished piece
to light he did not have,
to lacquered shine.

His muteness makes other tools
for speech. We talk
by printing letters in his hand,
his answer a throaty murmur,
quick way to say the words got through,
like light that didn't shine but bounced
and sent a message back.

Diane, the friend who knows him best,
is his interpreter. She speaks to him
with fingers moving quickly on his palm.
Replying, his fingers fly on her hand
opened to take the touching of his talk.
Signs jump in her skin
reading the code's semaphore.

He sits as if deciding things alone,
a hand on the table, a hand on his knee.
His silent rhythms aren't the ones we feel.

He walks through our talk to the kitchen,
times things outside our ticking clock,
waits for Diane's hand on his shoulder,
sits easy, accepts what is near
and what is out of reach.
He knows the room he feels,
has put each thing in memory in place.
Chair. Soap. Switch. Cap. Knob. Key.

Cutter, joiner,
finisher who finds
the completed cabinet
buried in the heart of the tree,

> *May I too feel,*
> *in my work, at its end,*
> *such fine smooth shape*
> *completed, and may I hold*
> *the form that I must find*
> *in what the tree offers to my hands.*

## GRANDMOTHER

Her old hands hate their idleness. It tires
her worse than cooking meals for twenty men,
the years the harvest filled the bunkhouse beds
with hired help. Her eyes are two slow fires
that burn to see the ranch they worked again,
green fields threaded by the Beaverhead.

The ranch is now this room. The iron stove
she lit, cold mornings, five o'clock
or earlier, is gone, like every lamb
and hen. The valley that she fell in love
with, a Croatian girl of eighteen, tricks
her, leaving fast as trains from Ellis Island came.

The lightest load's the hardest one to bear.
The fields are grey mist when the sun goes down.
She dreams of what the ranch was like in fall,
and no one has an argument she'll hear.
She sleeps, and ninety years tell her at dawn
she should get up to light the stove there still.

## STRAND AVENUE

I think of her light footsteps at the house
in summer shoes, the warm light of July,
the garden ripened to its prime, a day's
light work of summer chores like shelling peas
for supper and the snap of green cracked pods,
when supper was the yield that morning picked
and carried to the kitchen from the sod –
zucchini, carrots, beans and corn to shuck.
Light sat on the round backs of the mountains
and the receding ridge to Lolo Pass.
A task was always painting the old fence,
the line that framed the furrows and the grass.
There was a swinging gate that let things go
and opened in on what we used to know.

## FOR ANDREA

You wanted music and the airy form
of dance, and lifted footsteps set in light
and motion practised like a ruthless norm,
until your feet were like a bird's, in flight
and sound, until Tchaikovsky satisfied,
would let you rest in what your steps achieved.
This was your faith as if you had denied
yourself the earth as something to believe.
I watched your early steps and saw the dance
you wanted taking shape in you, the prize
it was, the reaching capture and the trance,
the way you felt your lifted body rise
in music, as you, leaping, twisting, turned
to music and your lighted figure burned.

## ALICE

I met you in the dark, and in a crowd,
free, waiting to see what fate would arrange,
that first night at college, us, milling, loud,
the strange Gothic quad feeling less strange
as we hung about in the noise and crush.
Whatever put you near us, it was you
that answered, when Jack asked what was happening,
some teasing thing – it wasn't that you knew –
your joke began the year when everything
was new, and studied in the pouring rush
that pulled you nearer from that silly night
we met, a bunch of us tramped the city,
then weeks, unsettled, settled, books, the sight
of you that asked for your proximity.

## BLACK ROOK

for Paul Crowley

It's summer here, but one black rook
is roosting in the tree.
We wait for the call that will not come
from the cemetery. On holiday
in this city of your great ambivalence,
ringed by the brooding mountains you hated,
we ramble the streets near your house.
No more of your spleen
about your Gothic bedridden mother,
your father's suave, professional absence,
your pharmaceutical brother,
the house where you avoided one another,
and sought allegiances elsewhere.
Your family seemed useful only
as a source of jokes for friends,
when you would deny you were lonely,
an inner exile from the wilderness outpost
of a city that closes early to hunt
or fish or ride a cycle to a bar.
Convert to astronomy, you drove us to a field
one night, and tipped us at the stars.
In disbelief, we put beer cans to our eyes,
and laughed at Sirius, the Pleiades,
Cassiopeia, some twenty-five years ago.

Here, now, in the dark, under the lights
with radiant names that hang over the mountains,
I think of you with us that night,
driving us out in your station wagon
to the sunken field behind the hill
to distances you wanted us to see.

## FOR JENNIFER

Rehearsing, we'd take places to recite
music to shadows in the sanctuary,
dark rafters over us, in the stalls' light.
The discipline of sound would settle all
to listening to the sixteenth century
come back in our voices, if all went well.

Good nights felt echoes. Memory and time
rehearsed the progress of a ritual,
followed the hill path of a pulsing psalm,
combined the voices in a bright motet,
poured hymns, practised a funeral, until
music forgot the time in search of it.

Now you have disappeared into the sound,
a voice that weighed the sadness that it sang,
schooled in the score, a voice that lived to bring
a line to its crescendo, fade, and then
to feel the bright motif come back again.
And music makes a silence when it ends.

So now in sound a slow procession brings
due mourning ceremony down the nave,
offering the ritual which you must have.
Our coming is your going. If this rings
true, you are wearing your blue choral gown
and stones are singing as we lay you down.

## TIME IN THE BEAVERHEAD VALLEY

It ticked the clouds across a valley field.
The sun and rain that fed the valley turned
in its brass wheels, and the mechanics held
the settled rhythm of the ranch that earned
a yield from weather changing like the clock
that turns the sun and stars. These little wheels
made clockwork of the wagons and the knock
that set the posts in fields, would give and steal
each hour that grew the barley, pushed the stream,
and calved when it came time. It made a count
of spring and harvest, winter and the wind.
It rounded with the round hills when they dreamed.
It pulled the plough like horses with its sound.
Brass ticking moved what happened in the ground.

## HAYING

We start out telling jokes,
working across the new-mown field.
An easy pace in hands and feet:
two walk behind the truck, one drives;
the walkers stack the wagon bed.
Hay stubble bristles under foot.

Rain's made the numbers good.
We load a neat geometry,
eighteen across by four bales wide,
four high. The axles creak
with this square profit from the sun.

The barn is like a gaping lung
of thick alfalfa dust.
We shake it from our hair and cough,
wearing green chaff like cloth.

The loading done, we lean and talk.
Now let it rain.
The sky's grey moods can fall.
We've pulled the field inside.

## MISSOULA FARMERS' MARKET

The market here has fallen from the air,
and run out of the earth to these tables
where stalls are banking money from the sun.
The rain and heat can make a sharp spade rich.

A simple business, digging green provender
out of the opened wallet of the earth.
The lush profusion slows the passing eye
to spilling heaps for summer's appetite.

Soil's green luxury tempts the hand
to stop and lift the smell of fresh-picked thyme
and hold a clutch of leafy rosemary and
shaggy basil, wet with the dew on the stems.

We lock our bikes by bright striped canopies
that sprouted overnight by the bridge
where a girl and a guy with guitars
are singing to the awakened morning.

At berries my hands are birds on the clusters;
the taste anticipated makes the purchase.
A girl a fifth the size of her father
assists him with blackberry eyes.

And flowers, sheaves of snow-white hyacinths,
and peonies, hibiscus, purple lavender.
Other stalls are a soup in the making,
blood red tomatoes, leeks and celery.

Honey, lifted from blossoms by the bees,
their rest in the petals that moment's theft,
stands in clear glass jars with a price on it.

A farm is bundled into small cloth bags.

How can we carry all this home,
out of the press of the crowd? But we do,
bags of it, fingers aching in the grip,
the music fading behind us.

My handlebars smell of basil,
bunched wet green that rubs the air.

## THE OXFORD CLUB

Round shoulders line up at the bar and brood.
Old boredom's bought its beer in here for years,
kept elbow distance from the same old jokes,
and told the unemployed that anywhere
is better than the street.
Comfort's a small, half-mumbled thing,
and listening tires the barmaid's smile.

The barmaid's angry with the grey old man
who stands and leans across the counter.
She bangs the beer fridge door and shouts at him;
he slouches in a docile haze and grins.
He's sleepy drunk but tries to be polite.
He wants a cab. She grabs the phone and calls,
then barks at him to wait, hands angry with the cloth
that swabs the white linoleum. She rolls her eyes:
she's got worse problems on her mind.
She laughs, pretending she's forgotten him.
The cab arrives, and out the old man goes,
shuffles across the sidewalk to the open door,
hand up for shield against the sun,
and slams himself inside.

## BLIND RIVER

Nothing to tell
why they abandoned
the grey wooden house,
who built it large enough
to raise a family,
a mile from town on the river,
or why they closed the door
and never went back into it.

It is as if the windows tired
of watching ripples passing on the stream,
as if the heavy, sluggish, moving shape
persuaded everyone inside to move,
until they finally succumbed and left.

Wind turned the house
the grey of river sand.
Nothing but darkness harbours there.
The wind returns it
to the river's fluid purposes.

## MEDICINE WHEEL

A narrow road climbed mountain shoulders
along a ledge in the upper air,
heaving thin breath on wind-scoured walls.

The ruts narrowed and petered out
to a stony track, no more than a path for deer or sheep,
our backs bent to difficult steps.

The top we came to was plate-flat,
a scoured open shelf noisy with wind,
a rough, high, level place, a rock face
tipped at the sky and the buffeting push
of the air, the constant beating sweep
that knocked against the kicking apex
that we reached.

We surveyed the open circle of the stones
set in this upper space
like a cemetery in the wind's force,
marker stones in an altitude
as strange as a promise to clouds,
language uttered by the ground.

Belief, I know, could find beginning here,
where everything below the mountain kneels.
I think about the purpose of a wheel
that sleeps in stillness, where
there is no need to move.

## WYOMING

Wyoming wrinkles into clefts and heights
as we drive into it, and rivers slip
and seep through rounded valley bowls of light.
We climb a gorge. The highway crawls and drops.
We move like insects down the valley line
inside the huge permission of the air,
less than a shadow's footprint where cliffs loom
like weather's giant chambers and great doors.
It seems to me the world is opening
to wider spaces than the eye can hold,
and we are in this moment happening
across a place where vastness will expand
as we move into it, a road that winds
along a river, bending where it bends.

## CHRISTMAS

The jets' rush starts the miracle: we fly,
lift-off of a hundred tons,
so many we could be a little town
cradled in aluminum.

We eat peanuts in the sky.
We fall asleep
between the earth and the moon.

We drop at night like angels
into Minneapolis, that lies
like a million scattered
candles in the snow.

## AT THE GUGGENHEIM

As if all history and art were full of birds,
a man is playing jazz, and he's found
rapture like wings in his hands.
It fills the building. We climb
Frank Lloyd Wright's wide spiral
up 5,000 years of Chinese art,
three stern terra cotta soldiers keeping watch,
a horse beside them just about to move.
We see blue polished jade, and figurines
unearthed from graves and smiling, a wine flask
with a blue design sweeter than drunkenness
beside a laughing King of Heaven in a small glass case,
a goose-shaped lamp holding a fish,
a dragon coiled in a bowl like soup for the mind,
and then, our two hours up, a jade official,
no older after twenty centuries,
complies with the guard who tells us
we've had our time,
and must go back out to the streets
that make their own wild, many-handed jazz all night.

## BLUES BAR

for Guy Davis and Jordan Berg

Whatever hunger draws the crowd tonight,
they clearly like the bar
and the songs a bluesman
pushes through the smoke.
The place is packed: they dance,
crowd the tables, lean against a wall.
The girls in front of me – a baseball team,
a bowling league, or just a bunch
that figured the bar was it tonight?
The girls love everything.
On stage it's just his songs
and his guitar. The patterns in his fingers
make what's jumping in the room.
He sings "The Georgia Flood."
A black disaster floats across the bar
and we drift with it,
remembering, forget.
The girls keep dancing and he moves the room.

The girls keep dancing.
Anyone can see, for them, tonight,
the music's better than a stream
of strikes and hits.
They feel the room's close smoky happiness.
For now, the bluesman's hands and voice
are everything. The night gets thick.
We pray his hands don't tire.
Songs take us into trouble
and back out of it.

## HAMLET

He came to cool oblivion
as if it couldn't wait,
poor victim in a royal game
he understood too late.

Most memorable in his complaints,
he watched them congregate
and measuring the depth of them,
he bent to take their weight.

He settled with his enemies
and gave them their release,
then stepped to death himself and took
the offered terms of peace.

He thought life's sweetest offering
a half-proved postulate,
his mind a court of premises
that trapped him in debate.

He railed against his prison house
though sentence there was brief,
and left as his memorial
the palace of his grief.

## LADY MACBETH

Lady Macbeth is resting in the park:
she is already wearing black.
Others gather, gossip.
She lies on a bench, private,
quiet, practising monarchy.

She knows what she has to say:
she has rehearsed the knife.
Resting, she enjoys shadows
under the shaggy trees,
the late afternoon as it cools.

Military banners flout the sky.
Speakers mounted in the trees
will startle the weather.
Thunder will shock the squirrels.
A stiff breeze blows from the lake.

The lake, we know, is very deep:
its depths are cold.
She has the knife beside her.
Resting, she feels the cold
of that deep water reaching her.

## THE AFTERLIFE

*The afterlife, do you believe in it?*
The question came up at the bar
and deepened our agenda
on a snowy night.
One of us wished to believe,
like his parents. One of us
was categorical. *You die, that's it, you're done,*
*carbon in the ground.* Proved this with a story:
said he put his father's ashes in the ground,
felt nothing, lowered the urn, set him down,
felt no electric flash.
This stilled the beer at our lips.
They took my silence
for agreement. I leaned back,
wanting hope, and remembered
my own cold mornings
inside a cemetery's gates
but could not somehow then
give my own account.
Death seemed a good long stretch
from where we were that night,
and if, for me,
the moment was a muted podium,
I relished the noisy interference all around me
the distance to the final, lettered stone.
Relished also, that cold night,
the ease of ordering one more
by raising my empty bottle.

## THE PENNINE WAY

for Kenneth Hillier and Michael Harper

I go out, interpreting hills,
nosing direction from a fence.
The slope, on looking back,
makes the village toys in the valley's bag.

The bare hill
is five minutes' home
in a moment of sun.
The cloud over a hill
is a white hill.
My eye rests.

Morning's work is
proving the guidebook true
to a stony path.
I read the ground, listening
to the air murmur
the purpose that put these
places on a Roman map.
I walk half lost
treading by streams
in freedom that aims
at a long Roman wall.

At night I climb down
from the line I followed
through glum hills
and the clouds' high silence
to the hostel, to close quarters,
beer, and at my elbow, talk thick as rain.

## NIGHT FISHERMEN ON BRONTE PIER

The wooden wharf has drowned and disappeared.
Now concrete jetties, wide smooth parallels,
hold back the lake's incoming moods.
Fishing boats that tied up in the twenties
sail ghost waters in old photographs
when perch, trout, salmon, ice-packed for New York,
peopled the clapboard shanties on the wharf,
the sagging deck awash in gutted slime.

The pier's become a walk for holidays,
stretches out warm evenings in the spring
and benches are the rest of squalling gulls.
Developers moor condominiums
that tower along the shore like boats aground.
High floors of lake-ward windows glaze the view.
Coffee shops draw idlers to boutiques
and talk settles into patios like nests.

A bright-lit gallery has drifted in
next door to glossy real estate offices,
salons as bare and functional as banks
where posted ads lure waterbirds to perch
on a more permanent basis by the lake.
A sales pitch teaches sandals to feel sand.
A wine bar and umbrellas sell the shade.
On good wine tables drift away like sails.

You can buy lingerie on the new river,
and paper mâché parrots on a pole.
In restaurants the best meal is the lake
served to your table soon as you sit down.
But on the water about one a.m.,
on a Tuesday in November,

nothing floats except the wrinkled moon.
The wind returns old worries to the pier.

On canvas stools wrapped shapes in parkas
trade cigarettes and fish the huddled dark.
Their sport is sun's antithesis.
The moon's eye watches their uncertainties
that promise nothing but sluggish freighters
crawling the horizon. Jokes bait the air,
and cigarettes throw wide a moment's net
that hangs in the air and dissipates.

Time swims away. They count the night
in silvers if there's luck, in good jokes
if there's not. Wind sags in willow breaks
catching dry leaves. Luck may get nothing more.

Photo: Mina Da Costa

Hamish Guthrie was born in Toronto, studied English and philosophy at the University of Toronto, and taught high school English and drama in Oakville, Ontario. His poems have appeared in Canada, the US, and Britain in publications such as *The Yale Literary Magazine, The Fiddlehead, Queen's Quarterly and Malahat. Undercurrents* (Cormorant Books 2011) included nine of his poems. He often holidays with his wife in her home state, Montana.

Thanks for purchasing this book and for supporting authors and artists. As a token of gratitude, please scan the QR code for exclusive content from this title.

**Please enjoy these other great titles from At Bay Press:**

*Pistachios in My Pocket*
by Sareh Farmand
Poetry
$24.95
ISBN 9781988168692
Available now

*Trees*
by Lucy Hemphill
Illustrations by Michael Joyal
Poetry
$24.95
ISBN 9781988168289
Available now

*Sun Compass*
by Brigette DePape
Poetry
$24.95
ISBN 9781988168616
Available now

*Occasionally Petty*
by Michelle Lietz
Poetry
$24.95
ISBN 9781988168593
Available now

*Through Disassembled House of Perfect Stones*
by David Yerex Williamson
Poetry
$24.95
ISBN 9781988168692
Available now

*Moving Upstream*
by Mary Barnes
Poetry
$24.95
ISBN 9781988168593
Spring 2023